BRING
IN THE
HOLLY

Poems for Christmas by
Charles Causley

with illustrations by
Lisa Kopper

FRANCES LINCOLN

To Margaret and Reg Huzzey

Text copyright © 1992 Charles Causley
Illustrations copyright © 1992 Lisa Kopper

Acknowledgements
The following poems were previously published in Great Britain,
and grateful acknowledgement is made to the publishers:
for 'The Animals' Carol' and 'Ballad of the Bread Man' from
Collected Poems 1951-75 (Macmillan London Ltd., 1975); for
'A Song of Truth' from *A Field of Vision* (Macmillan London Ltd., 1988);
for 'At Nine of the Night I Opened My Door' from *Figgie Hobbin*
(Macmillan Children's Books Ltd., 1970); for 'Angels' Song'
and 'Mary's Song' from *The Gift of a Lamb* (Robson Books Ltd., 1978).

Bring in the Holly first published in Great Britain in 1992 by
Frances Lincoln Limited, Apollo Works
5 Charlton Kings Road, London NW5 2SB

British Library Cataloguing in Publication Data
available on request

ISBN 0-7112-0668-6

Printed and bound in Hong Kong

1 3 5 7 9 8 6 4 2

Contents

They're Fetching in Ivy and Holly

'They're fetching in ivy and holly
And putting it this way and that.
I simply can't think of the reason,'
Said Si-Si the Siamese cat.

'They're pinning up lanterns and streamers.
There's mistletoe over the door.
They've brought in a tree from the garden.
I do wish I knew what it's for.

'It's covered with little glass candles
That go on and off without stop.
They've put it to stand in a corner
And tied up a fairy on top.

'They're stringing bright cards by the dozen
And letting them hang in a row.
Some people outside in the roadway
Are singing a song in the snow.

'I saw all the children write letters
And – I'm not at all sure this was wise –
They posted each one *up the chimney*.
I couldn't believe my own eyes.

'What on earth, in the middle of winter,
Does the family think it is at?
Won't somebody please come and tell me?'
Said Si-Si the Siamese cat.

At Nine of the Night I Opened My Door

At nine of the night I opened my door
That stands midway between moor and moor,
And all around me, silver-bright,
I saw that the world had turned to white.

Thick was the snow on field and hedge
And vanished was the river-sedge,
Where winter skilfully had wound
A shining scarf without a sound.

And as I stood and gazed my fill
A stable-boy came down the hill.
With every step I saw him take
Flew at his heel a puff of flake.

His brow was whiter than the hoar,
A beard of freshest snow he wore,
And round about him, snowflake starred,
A red horse-blanket from the yard.

In a red cloak I saw him go,
His back was bent, his step was slow,
And as he laboured through the cold
He seemed a hundred winters old.

I stood and watched the snowy head,
The whiskers white, the cloak of red.
'A Merry Christmas!' I heard him cry.
'The same to you, old friend,' said I.

A Song of Truth

When Christ the Lord of Heaven was born
Cold was the land.
His mother saw along the road
A fig-tree stand.
'Good Mary, leave the figs to grow
For we have thirty miles to go.
The hour is late.'

Mary came near unto the town.
Stayed at a door.
Said to the little farmer, 'Pray
Let us stay here.
Not for myself these words I make
But for an infant child's sake.
The night is chill.'

The farmer opened up his barn.
Bade them go in.
When half the winter night had gone
Came there again.
'Where you are from in this wide world,
And are not killed by winter cold,
I cannot tell.'

The farmer came into his house
The barn beside.
'Rise up, dear wife,' he cried, 'and may
Best fire be made
That these poor travellers are warm
And safe from wind and weather's harm
Here at our hearth.'

Smiling, Mary then entered in
The farmhouse door;
Also her good and gentle man
That self-same hour
Drew from his pack a crock of tin,
With snow the young child filled it fine,
And it was flour.

Crystals of ice he placed therein
As sugar rare
And water that white milk should be
Both fresh and fair.
Over the flame they hung the crock,
And such soft sweetness did they cook,
Was finest pap.

Of wooden chip the good man carved
With homely blade
A spoon that was of ivory
And diamond made.
And now the child does Mary sweet
Give of the pap that He may eat:
Jesus his name.

translated from the German

9

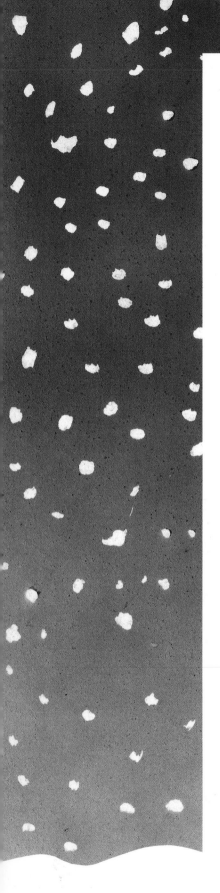

Parson's Lea

That Christmas we went carolling
Over at Parson's Lea:
Barnaby Bly, Sam and Sal Spry,
Mickey McGee and me.

Said Sammy, 'We're sure of a dollar
If we sing out sweet and fine,
And cakes and pies to dazzle your eyes
And glasses of home-made wine!'

So quiet we came to Parson's Lea
And nobody heard us come.
The trees they leaned and the scritch-owl screamed
And my heart began to drum.

Up we went to Parson's Lea
And never a star did shine,
By the graveyard wall and the tower tall
And the church clock telling nine.

We started on *Good King Wenceslas*
But Barnaby pitched it high
And Sally she wriggled and Sammy he giggled
And Mickey began to cry.

Down came a bucket of water
That wetted us to the skin,
And that was our fee at Parson's Lea
And nobody asked us in.

As we went home by the Ridgeway
Barney and Mick turned blue
And Sal she quivered and Sam he bivered
And I was shivering too,

When out of her cottage doorway
There looked old Jennifer Starr.
'Come in,' she said, 'for it's half of dead
And cold and tired you are.

'Sit yourselves down by the fireside
And give yourselves a bake.'
And as soon as we sat by Tom the cat
She brought out A CHRISTMAS CAKE.

She gave to us each an orange,
A drink that was hot and neat,
And a little man made of marzipan –
The best we ever did eat.

'Will you sing *King Wenceslas*?' she said.
'There's nothing that I'd like more!'
And for Jennifer Starr we sang better by far
Than ever we sang before.

Now Jenny has slept in her green bed
Fifty years and ten,
But I see her clear with her Christmas cheer
As the day I saw her then.

And Barnaby Bly is a banker,
Sammy's as skint as Job,
And Mickey McGee ran off to sea
And was seven times round the globe.

Sally she married a soldier
Came from the U.S.A.
And not a word has one of us heard
From Sal since she went away.

But in the dark of winter
When Christmas comes again,
Every year I'm certain sure
We remember it plain as plain –

Barnaby Bly, Sam and Sal Spry,
Mickey McGee and me:
The Christmas we went carolling
Over at Parson's Lea.

Christmas at Les Baux

Angels, under elm and lotus
On St Vincent Square
Adjust a drifted wing, a halo.
Fix their gold hair.

Shepherds, caped and scarved for winter
From field are come;
Gather at the church door, sounding
Squealing fife, the drum.

See the small cart hung with greening
Drawn by the ram;
Safe in straw and soft hay lying
The new-born lamb.

Now among the winking candles,
Shadowed stone and painted glass
Breaks the Christmas hymn at midnight
As they pass.

Fierce the moonlight, fierce the starlight
Burn on crag and scree.
Deep below, the river reaches
For the sea.

In the town of rock, of ruin
Slung between the sky, the plain,
Hear the voicing, the rejoicing.
Christ is born again.

*The ceremony described here still takes place
on Christmas Eve in the French hill-town
of Les Baux en Provence.*

12

The Animals' Carol

Christus natus est! the cock Carols on the morning dark.	Christ is born
Quando? croaks the raven stiff Freezing on the broken cliff.	When?
Hoc nocte, replies the crow Beating high above the snow.	This night
Ubi? Ubi? booms the ox From its cavern in the rocks.	Where?
Bethlehem, then bleats the sheep Huddled on the winter steep.	Bethlehem
Quomodo? the brown hare clicks, Chattering among the sticks.	How?
Humiliter, the careful wren Thrills upon the cold hedge-stone.	Humbly
Cur? Cur? sounds the coot By the iron river-root.	Why?
Propter homines, the thrush Sings on the sharp holly-bush.	For the sake of man
Cui? Cui? rings the chough On the strong, sea-haunted bluff.	To whom?
Mary! Mary! calls the lamb From the quiet of the womb.	Mary
Praeterea ex quo? cries The woodpecker to pallid skies.	Who else?
Joseph, breathes the heavy shire Warming in its own blood-fire.	Joseph

Ultime ex quo? the owl Solemnly begins to call.	Who above all?
De Deo, the little stare Whistles on the hardening air.	Of God
Pridem? Pridem? the jack snipe From the harsh grass starts to pipe.	Long ago?
Sic et non, answers the fox Tiptoeing the bitter lough.	Yes and no
Quomodo hoc scire potest? Boldly flutes the robin redbreast.	How do I know this?
Illo in eandem, squeaks The mouse within the barley-sack.	By going there
Quae sarcinae? asks the daw Swaggering from head to claw.	What luggage?
Nulla res, replies the ass, Bearing on its back the Cross.	None
Quantum pecuniae? shrills The wandering gull about the hills.	How much money?
Ne nummum quidem, the rook Caws across the rigid brook.	Not a penny
Nulla resne? barks the dog By the crumbling fire-log.	Nothing at all?
Nil nisi cor amans, the dove Murmurs from its house of love.	Only a loving heart

Gloria in Excelsis! Then
Man is God, and God is Man.

Ballad of the Bread Man

Mary stood in the kitchen
   Baking a loaf of bread.
An angel flew in through the window.
   'We've a job for you,' he said.

'God in his big gold heaven,
   Sitting in his big blue chair,
Wanted a mother for his little son.
   Suddenly saw you there.'

Mary shook and trembled,
   'It isn't true what you say.'
'Don't say that,' said the angel.
   'The baby's on its way.'

Joseph was in the workshop
   Planing a piece of wood.
'The old man's past it,' the neighbours said.
   'That girl's been up to no good.'

'And who was that elegant fellow,'
   They said, 'in the shiny gear?'
The things they said about Gabriel
   Were hardly fit to hear.

Mary never answered,
   Mary never replied.
She kept the information,
   Like the baby, safe inside.

It was election winter.
   They went to vote in town.
When Mary found her time had come
   The hotels let her down.

The baby was born in an annexe
   Next to the local pub.
At midnight, a delegation
   Turned up from the Farmers' Club.

They talked about an explosion
   That made a hole in the sky,
Said they'd been sent to the Lamb & Flag
   To see God come down from on high.

A few days later a bishop
   And a five-star general were seen
With the head of an African country
   In a bullet-proof limousine.

'We've come,' they said, 'with tokens
   For the little boy to choose.'
Told the tale about war and peace
   In the television news.

After them came the soldiers
   With rifle and bomb and gun,
Looking for enemies of the state.
   The family had packed and gone.

When they got back to the village
   The neighbours said, to a man,
'That boy will never be one of us,
   Though he does what he blessed well can.'

He went round to all the people
   A paper crown on his head.
Here is some bread from my father.
   Take, eat, he said.

Nobody seemed very hungry.
   Nobody seemed to care.
Nobody saw the god in himself
   Quietly standing there.

He finished up in the papers.
   He came to a very bad end.
He was charged with bringing the living to life.
   No man was that prisoner's friend.

There's only one kind of punishment
 To fit that kind of a crime.
They rigged a trial and shot him dead.
 They were only just in time.

They lifted the young man by the leg,
 They lifted him by the arm,
They locked him in a cathedral
 In case he came to harm.

They stored him safe as water
 Under seven rocks.
One Sunday morning he burst out
 Like a jack-in-the-box.

Through the town he went walking.
 He showed them the holes in his head.
Now do you want any loaves? he cried.
 'Not today,' they said.

Three Kings

(I) *Out of the East*
Out of the east three Kings came riding
Bright in the light of the sun and moon,
High in the sky a star their guiding:
Gold in the night and silver at noon.

Through the green forest and over the river,
Valley of ice and desert of flame,
Onward they rode their truth to discover,
Led by a star with never a name.

(II) *Three Lamps Burned*
Three lamps burned in the midnight sky,
One was low and one was high,
One was far and then was nigh;
Three lamps burned as bright as the sun –
     Then they were one,
     They were one.

Three men journeyed then as one
Led by a light as strong as the sun.
Morning and noon and night it shone
Over their heads on the joyful road
     To a King and God,
     King and God.

(III) *Swift through the Night Sky*
Swift through the night sky swims a star
Over the Kings who journey far –
     Incense and myrrh and gold in hand
     Over the white and winter land.

Incense and gold and myrrh they bear
Through the sharp seasons of the air;
     Three good gifts the Wise Men bring:
     Gold for the earth and heaven's king,

Myrrh for an infant born to die,
Frankincense for a godhead high –
      Under a star that glows like a gem,
      Pointing the road to Bethlehem.

See where it shines and now is still
Over the house that stands on the hill;
      The door is open, the window clear
      To welcome the Wise Men who now are near,
      Now are near,
      Now are here.

(IV) *Three Wise Men to the Sea came Down*

Three Wise Men to the sea came down,
Sailed in a ship from Tarshish town.
      Herod may rail and Herod roar,
      Never did he see them more,
      Never more,
      Never more,
      Never did he see them more.

Over the stones and over the sand
Jesus rode into Egypt land.
      Herod may rail and Herod roar,
      Never did he see them more,
      Never more,
      Never more,
      Never did he see them more.

This is a tale of days long gone,
But still for us the star shines on.
      Herods may rail and Herods roar,
      But the star will shine for evermore,
      Evermore,
      Evermore,
      The star will shine for evermore.

Christmas Pudding

Christmas pudding,
    Christmas cracker,
Christmas turkey,
    Christmas tree,
They all sat down together
    And were sad as sad could be
For Christmas-time was coming
    And they felt for certain sure
By Christmas night things wouldn't quite
    Be as they were before.

'I wish you hadn't told me,'
    The Christmas pudding said,
'They'll boil me in a pan and stick
    Some holly in my head,
And after Christmas dinner
    (This is the bit I hate)
There's not a plum or pudding crumb
    On anybody's plate.'

'It's clear enough,' the turkey huffed,
    'For anyone to see
When I say *Hobble! Gobble!*
    I don't mean gobble me.
But bless my feathers, bless my beak,
    When Christmas Day has flown,
I've heard what's left of this poor bird
    Is only skin and bone.'

'I can't deny,' the cracker cried,
    'I'm feeling rather blue
That all this red and green and gold
    Will soon be torn in two.
As for the rest, I must confess,
    It gives me such a pang
To know that by this time next week
    I've gone off with a bang.'

'Dear me,' then said the Christmas tree,
    'It makes me want to blub.
I hear they're going to pull me up
    And stand me in a tub.
And when the party's over
    And my needles dropped and dead,
They'll throw me on the rubbish heap
    Behind the garden shed.'

Said the turkey to the pudding
    And the cracker and the tree,
'Though Christmas is a jolly time
    And fills most folk with glee,
It's something rather different
    For you, my friends, and me –
And just what must become of us
    Is all too plain to see.'

So the cracker and the turkey
    And the pudding and the tree
They all ran off together
    Over land and over sea.
They crossed the silver river
    And they crossed the snowy plain
And they crossed the ragged mountain
    And were never seen again.

And north or south or east or west
    In air or on the ground,
There's never been a sign of them
    And never been a sound
Since they crept across the meadow
    And they leapt across the lea,
Happy pudding,
                Happy cracker,
Happy turkey,
                Happy tree.

Angels' Song

FIRST ANGEL Fear not, shepherds, for I bring
Tidings of a new-born King –
Not in castle, not in keep,
Nor in tower strong and steep.
Not in manor-house or hall,
But a humble ox's stall.

SECOND ANGEL Underneath a standing star
And where sheep and cattle are,
In a bed of straw and hay
God's own Son is born this day.
If to Bethlehem you go,
This the truth you soon shall know.

THIRD ANGEL And as signal and as sign,
Sure as all the stars that shine,
You shall find him, shepherds all,
Swaddled in a baby-shawl;
And the joyful news will share
With good people everywhere.

SECOND ANGEL Therefore, listen as we cry:

THREE ANGELS Glory be to God on high,
And his gifts of love and peace
To his people never cease.

Driving Home

Driving home, in wrong weather,
Half-melted stars adrift
In a warmth of sky, the tin voice
Of the car radio sprinkling
Music for Spanish guitar,
I had forgotten, for some reason,
Time, place and season.

Then, suddenly, the church:
Lit granite lantern.
Coloured glass saints pointing
Stiff arms to pray or praise.
Over its ragged screen
Of elm, yew, oak,
The tower spoke.

As if at the push of dark
The door unclosed.
Men, women, children
In smiling light
Streamed a thin path between
Tomb and long-planted stone.
Headed for home.

Above, six bells (one cracked)
Thumped down the scale.
'Merry Christmas!' Tom, Jack
And Maisie called.
'Don't seem like Christmas.
More like Midsummer,'
They grinned one to another.

'Every day Christmas Day!'
They smelt of whisky and tobacco.
Climbed into the bent, half-spent van,
Making for Moor Farm
As I wondered what,
In all that Mediterranean air,
They should discover there.

Mary's Song

Sleep, King Jesus,
Your royal bed
Is made of hay
In a cattle-shed.
Sleep, King Jesus,
Do not fear,
Joseph is watching
And waiting near.

Warm in the wintry air
You lie,
The ox and the donkey
Standing by.
With summer eyes
They seem to say:
Welcome, Jesus,
On Christmas Day!

Sleep, King Jesus:
Your diamond crown
High in the sky
Where the stars look down.
Let your reign
Of love begin,
That all the world
May enter in.